The Great Permission

An Asset-Based Field Guide for Congregations

The Great Permission

An Asset-Based Field Guide for Congregations

Writer: Bob Sitze

Editor: Laurel Hensel

Designer: Kristina Meyer; Orangeflux, Inc.

Development Team:

         Tom Dudley

         Michael Meier

         Keith Mundy

         Kurt Nordby

         Nancy Snell

         Dick Stough

For a Spanish version of *The Great Permission*, see the resource, *Dones de Gracia: Una guía de acción para congregaciones (www.elca.org/stewardship/spanish.html)*

Table of Contents

How To

What's a "field book"?

Make this book your own.

What you're holding in your hands is a "field book," a resource to help you understand what you encounter on your journey as a congregational leader.

ABOUT THIS BOOK

This book is divided into two parts: a background section that provides scriptural and philosophical foundations for an asset-based approach, and a how-to section that gives specific helps for decisions and actions you might take. It's OK to jump ahead for concrete ideas about how this approach works.

Each two-page reading presents a single concept about asset thinking and planning. Together the readings reveal the terrain you'll encounter as you take an asset-based approach to congregational life.

USING THE BOOK

Imagine yourself in your "field" (your church council, your youth group, etc.) and what you hope will happen while you're there. Now you can think about how to use this book to:

❖ Name and shape what you face as a leader

❖ Know what to look for and what to avoid

❖ Move beyond worry or despair

❖ Assist you as you grow skilled in this approach

❖ Give you comfort when facing something unfamiliar

❖ Assure you that you may already know this field and that you can take advantage of being here.

THE BOOK IS YOURS

Make this book your own in any way that helps. Dog-ear the pages you like, make notes in the margins, take pages to meetings, pray about what you read, or stuff additional materials between the pages you like.

Enjoy using this book about the field of asset-based planning. Remember that God is already there and the Holy Spirit will accompany you.

ANOTHER LOOK

IF YOU LOOK FOR GOD'S GRACE, YOU CAN SEE IT EVERYWHERE. NOT SURPRISINGLY, EVEN THE GIFT OF BEING ABLE TO SEE WHERE GOD BLESSES THE WORLD IS AN EVIDENCE OF GRACE.

Grace is where to start

This book starts and ends with God's grace.

"Grace" is who God is. Grace is God's work. Bound up in Jesus Christ, grace is where your loving God starts looking at you. "Undeserved favor" could be God's nickname.

Amazing stuff, this grace from God. It shows itself in the free gift of salvation. Jesus paid for it already! But grace also appears in creation—in the amazing array of abilities and opportunities God has given in the world around and inside of you. (They're called "assets" in this book.) Grace shows up in every moment the Holy Spirit blesses you with God's wisdom, the forgiveness of sins, or a life of meaning and purpose.

You're saved and blessed and graced away from selfishness. You're graced and washed clean so that you can go about your life as a steward of God's grace. You're newly created so that you can give your life away!

Like everything else in the Christian faith, *The Great Permission* starts with God's grace. From this first page to the last, this book is dedicated to the notion that God's grace soaks every action in every congregation like the delicious chewing of berries indelibly coats your tongue and tints your teeth.

In *The Great Permission* you'll find God's grace under the words, inside the ideas, dancing with your sense of who God wants you to be. This book starts and ends with God's grace. Just like your life.

ANOTHER LOOK

LUTHER SNOW, AN ASSET-BASED COMMUNITY DEVELOPER IN IOWA, THINKS OF GOD'S GRACE AS THE GLUE THAT CONNECTS ASSETS SO THAT THEY GATHER TOGETHER FOR GOD'S PURPOSES.

"Acid" in our church?

"Acid" is a way of thinking that's full of complaints and over-neediness.

It's easy to confuse "asset" with "acid," especially when you're hearing the idea for the first time. This book is about how you can think and plan for your life and for your congregation, beginning with the assets God has given you, not with the acid that can eat away at your willingness to work toward God's purposes in your life or congregation.

This approach to being the church is based on a simple premise: When you start with a view of your life as "half-full," you will accomplish a lot more than if you think of your life as primarily "half-empty." In other words, when you realize you have enough, you're more likely to get to work than if you think you don't have nearly enough. Remember: God has blessed you so abundantly that your cup overflows.

"Acid" in the church's life—maybe even in your own—comes from continually trying to digest spiritual bile. "Acid" is a way of thinking that's full of complaints and over-neediness. It sounds whiny and it focuses on what is not possible. That kind of acid isn't good for people or congregations.

Simply put: an asset-based approach counteracts the acid that might sometimes undermine your life or your congregation's vitality. Its possibilities push aside any preoccupation with problems. Its joys help dispel worry and fear. This way of thinking and behaving helps God's people move past problems toward real opportunities.

And when you're finished reading this book, you'll hear "asset" every time we say the word.

ANOTHER LOOK

HAVE YOU EXPERIENCED "ACID" SENSATIONS LIKE FATIGUE, ANXIETY, DREAD OR GRIM RESIGNATION? WHAT MAY BE EATING AT YOU IS THE SUSPICION THAT YOU DON'T HAVE WHAT YOU NEED TO ACCOMPLISH SOMETHING IMPORTANT. THAT'S AN "ACID-BASED APPROACH!"

Getting started

This book is full of asset questions and answers.

Although asset-based thinking and planning are not easily captured in 10 easy steps, you can get started toward asset-based approaches in any of these ways:

PRAY DEEPLY. This approach may not be easy, but when you start to feel that it's the right way to go, you'll find that it matches the deeply yearning prayers you've sent to God. Keep praying that way.

"START OVER" WITH PEOPLE YOU'VE BEEN WORKING WITH. Have a heart-to-heart with them about some of your frustrations with needs-based approaches to congregational life. Be honest, not only about the futility you face, but also the hopes you harbor down deep.

START SMALL. Pick something simple, like the annual church picnic. Try an asset-based approach to plan something familiar. Along the way, talk about the possibilities you sense in this approach. (See Case Study 6.)

START NEW. Try an asset-based approach on something new in your congregation, like calling a new pastor, or starting a new program. Maybe even start with new people.

ASK "ASSET QUESTIONS" AND EXPECT "ASSET ANSWERS." This book is full of asset questions and answers. Pick some of your favorites, and keep asking them.

READ AND TALK ABOUT THIS BOOK. Read especially pertinent sections of this book, and talk about what you read with someone you trust or admire. Have the conversation in a comfortable location.

ANOTHER LOOK

ONE WAY TO GET STARTED: PICK A CASE STUDY IN THIS BOOK THAT'S LIKE YOUR SITUATION. TALK ABOUT ITS ELEMENTS, AND HOW IT'S SIMILAR OR DIFFERENT FROM YOUR CONGREGATION. THEN DECIDE WHAT TO DO NEXT.

Background

Using this section

Before you head out for the "field," you might want to spend time getting ready. In this section you'll find a series of two-page readings that help you:

❖ Learn the philosophical and practical fundamentals of the asset-based approach ("Other ways to say 'asset'").

❖ See the theological basis for "asset-based approaches" ("Grace gives permission").

❖ Think about some biblical foundations for this approach ("How much bread?").

READING IS ENOUGH

You'll benefit just from reading and thinking about the ideas here. That alone may help you change the way you approach doing ministry.

READING WITH ACTIONS

On the other hand, you might want to bring together
a group of people for conversation about what you've
read, start devotional conversations in meetings
or write your reactions to what you read.

CASE STUDIES

Several case studies have been scattered throughout
this section. Read the studies and the comments
attached to them. Talk about how the situations
might apply to your congregation and what other
thoughts they bring to mind.

TAKING "ANOTHER LOOK"

Each reading includes these quickly read paragraphs
of questions, comments and suggestions. You might
begin your quest for "what to do next" here.

Grace squeezed out

Grace is undeserved and free, and God wants you to have it.

If you approach your thinking and planning with assets in mind, you're bound to find God's grace. Like the contents of a tube of toothpaste, grace can be found where you expect it and sometimes where you don't.

You most likely expect God's grace to come to you when you worship with other members of your congregation: a sermon, some hymns and songs with a good message, forgiveness of sins, prayers that touch your soul.

But what happens when you open your eyes just a little more to the possibility of God's grace? You find God's grace there, too:

❖ Surprising excellence inside an "ordinary person"

❖ Children who say something that wakes up everyone

❖ A seemingly disastrous event that reveals your congregation's ability to prosper in spite of circumstances

* "Problems" that turn themselves inside out to become opportunities

* An abundance of assets where you thought few existed.

As you think and plan in an asset-based way, always be aware that you are likely experiencing the toothpaste-like evidence of God's grace. Grace is undeserved and free, and God wants you to have it. It's also worth sharing with others by the way you live in Christ's name and according to his example.

ANOTHER LOOK

WHERE IN YOUR LIFE DO YOU FIND GOD'S GRACE? PERHAPS AMONG THOSE YOU KNOW WHO ALWAYS FIND IN ANY SITUATION SOMETHING GOOD AND GRACE-FILLED. WHEN DO YOU PRAY FOR GOD'S GRACE?

Grace gives permission

You don't have to wait for directions...

God's grace carries permission. You're allowed to try things on for size, to make mistakes, to lurch forward without extensive planning, to take charge instead of waiting. You're allowed to enjoy being God's steward.

The biggest "permission"? You get to stand alongside all the rest of us—we're called "the church"—and work with other asset-gifted people to do together what you could never accomplish alone. In the church, you get supported and loved and encouraged. You are forgiven. You learn to forgive.

Larry has been the custodian at his congregation for 23 years. Over that time he's learned an important lesson: you don't have to wait for directions in order to do a good job. Larry thinks the same way about his relationship with God. He knows what needs to be done and he does it—confessing sin, praying, extending kindness, being generous.

When it comes to "doing church," you can be like Larry. You don't have to wait. You have everything you need from God to start right now to do your part of God's great work in the world and in your church.

In taking an asset-based approach to how you live life, don't stop at "obedience" or "discipleship" as the final stages in Christian maturity. Be ready to accept the more difficult role of steward. Stewards accept God's invitation to move forward, using their best judgment to carry out God's plan for the world.

You can believe these words that come with God's blessing: "You have my permission!"

ANOTHER LOOK

A SUCCESSFUL AND CUSTOMER-FRIENDLY AIRLINE HAS REMINDED US FOR YEARS THAT WE HAVE PERMISSION TO "MOVE ABOUT THE COUNTRY." HOW MIGHT THAT WORK AS A MISSION STATEMENT FOR YOUR CONGREGATION?

Not gone and not forgotten

If you're a steward (you are!) you always have to deal with the prospect that the Owner (or Landlord) will be absent while you continue your faithful service.

In the asset-based approach, you acknowledge that reality—you're not waiting around for the Owner to come back. But you don't forget another reality: God doesn't leave stewards hanging high and dry.

When you're a steward (you are!) you understand that what remains present—you can hear it, see it, touch it—is the will of the Owner. As Owner, God wants to continue creating, redeeming and making things holy. God wants to continue rubbing out evil. God wants people to live in love. God has in mind that forgiveness will continue to overcome blame and guilt. You understand this as "God's will," and it's what you try to get done by the way you live your life.

You hear and see God's will because you understand your dependence on God's Word for your life's meaning. Jesus is the example. The Holy Spirit equips you for following that example. God continues to recreate you and the world around you so that Jesus' example can actually take place. You are surrounded by like-minded people of faith with a similar sense of life purpose.

When you're a steward (you are!) you're not left alone at all.

ANOTHER LOOK

JESUS PROMISES YOU THE SAME THING HE PROMISED HIS FOLLOWERS: "I WILL BE WITH YOU ALWAYS, EVEN UNTIL THE END OF THE WORLD" (MATTHEW 28:29 CEV). HOW'S THAT TRUE FOR YOU?

Saved from tiny minds

Kristen's brain hasn't shrunk; neither has her head. But what has gotten too small is her view of who she really is. She's started to get a "tiny mind" because she sometimes thinks that she's basically a little speck of humanity in God's eyes, in the estimation of other people or in her own mind. Sometimes she thinks that her congregation feels the same way about its own collected "mind." This is not good.

Tiny-mindedness appears every time you think you're weaker, dumber, less powerful or less capable than you really are. Or when all you think about is what's not good about you or your congregation.

In asset-based thinking and planning God can provide for you a way out of this small—and actually kind of self-absorbed—way of thinking. When you (or your congregation) start to think about the abundance of the Spirit's gifts, about God's overwhelming generosity to you—that's when you stop thinking small about yourself and your congregation.

When you start putting those assets to use in all the wonderful places you want to serve God, you don't have time for small-mindedness. You're having too much fun trying out those gifts in new ways; you're excited about the new parts of your mind that are humming along; you're using everything you know and can do.

And suddenly, you're saved from any small-minded notions about what God has done for you—or what God has in mind for you.

ANOTHER LOOK

A SURE SIGN YOU'RE MEASURING YOURSELF OR YOUR CONGREGATION WITH A TINY MIND: OVERUSE OF "JUST" AND "ONLY" WHEN DESCRIBING WHO YOU ARE OR WHAT YOU DO. A SURE SOLUTION: STOP TALKING THAT WAY!

An ancient composer

Asset-based thinking has been around a long time, but perhaps not always known by that name. A good example is the 17th century German Baroque composer Heinrich Schuetz.

Schuetz spent his formative years in the majestic courts and cathedrals of Venice, where he learned religious composition from the great Giovanni Gabrielli. In the grand worship styles of that part of the world, it was normal to hear and see double-choir motets, multi-voiced brass choirs and pipe organs at the front and back of cathedrals.

"Normal" changed, though, when Schuetz returned to his native Germany to write religious music for his church in Dresden. Germany was being ravaged by civil and religious wars that were to last for decades.

As Schuetz surveyed the musical assets of his war-torn surroundings, he found considerably fewer possibilities than in Italy. A congregation might have two bassoonists, a soprano with a small voice range, a violin missing one string and a duck with a banjo. Instead of bemoaning the "lack of musical acumen," Schuetz instead wrote three volumes of Sacred Symphonies—choral settings of scriptural texts that could be performed with limited musical assets.

□ **A HUMOROUS EXAGGERATION TO MAKE THE POINT.**

Although some of his writings echoed the expansive compositions of his teachers, Schuetz endeared himself to his constituency because he understood how to use the assets he found instead of waiting for just the right time, the right musicians or the right skills.

□ **IN ASSET-BASED THINKING, "THE RIGHT TIME" IS NOW, "THE RIGHT PLACE" IS HERE, AND "THE RIGHT PEOPLE" ARE WITH YOU NOW.**

For what it's worth, Heinrich Schuetz's spirit is alive in sacred music today!

□ **HOW MIGHT THIS SAME APPROACH TO WORSHIP OR MUSIC OCCUR IN YOUR CONGREGATION?**

Love trumps fear

Your first asset: God's unconditional love for you.

Maurice is president of his congregation. Fear paralyzes Maurice. Whole sections of his brain don't operate when fear or anxiety captures his life.

The same thing happens when Maurice's congregation lives fearfully. When the people around Maurice think and behave in fear—or anger, which usually accompanies fear—they're not as capable of thinking or behaving in other ways. In fact, the more they fear, the better they get at it!

Brain scientists know that an effective way out of fear is love. (Yes, you're right—John wrote about this in his first letter, "Perfect love casts out fear," 1 John 4:18a.) When fearful or angry, your brain is calmed by love you receive and love you give away. And when that love is expressed in personal conversation, fear is even less capable of taking over the way your brain reacts to its environment.

An asset-based approach to congregational life doesn't honor fear, anger or anxiety. Love and trust—toward God, others and yourself—can blossom when you take seriously your first asset: God's unconditional love for you. Fear diminishes when you accept the reality of God's loving generosity toward you, even though you don't deserve it. Your thinking and planning can proceed with minimal fear when you start with an overwhelming sense of your plentiful abilities and gifts.

Want to dispel fear and anger? Take Jesus' advice to heart: "Just as I have loved you, you also should love one another" (John 13:34b).

ANOTHER LOOK

CONSIDER STARTING GROUP PLANNING WITH "FEAR-ASSESSMENT" QUESTIONS FOR THE TEAM: WHAT ARE WE AFRAID OF HERE, REALLY? WHAT'S THE WORST THAT COULD HAPPEN? WHAT ASSETS DO WE HAVE TO OVERCOME THESE FEARS?

31

"Alone" is a myth

You are never, ever "alone"...

What is one of the easiest temptations to give in to? That you're all alone, that you're "the only one who has ever…" This temptation asks that you believe in a soul-weakening myth.

Still, when you're a leader in a congregation it can sometimes feel like you are the only one who:

❖ cares

❖ wants to work

❖ has a long-term commitment

❖ knows what you're doing

❖ understands the importance of what's happening here.

When you approach things with a needs-based approach, you can fall for that temptation like a moth falls for a light bulb. You can circle around your alone-ness until you beat your wings into dust and lose your ability to fly.

In an asset-based approach, you start with the task of assembling the assets of *all who have gathered*, no matter how few they are. One of the strengths of this way of thinking and behaving is that it gathers together in one place capabilities that no single individual can muster alone.

When you name and organize those assets, you come to see the beauty of Jesus' "vine and branches" word picture (John 15) or Paul's description of church-as-human-body (1 Corinthians 12 and Ephesians 4). When connected to Christ, your congregation taps into the Spirit of God, to Jesus' example. You bond and bridge with one another to create a whole that is always greater than the sum of its parts.

Remember that you are never, ever alone.

ANOTHER LOOK

EVEN THE STRONGEST AND MOST FAITHFUL LEADER SECRETLY WRESTLES WITH "ALONE" TEMPTATIONS. A GOOD WAY TO PROTECT AGAINST THOSE THOUGHTS: TALK WITH EACH OTHER ABOUT THE GOOD YOU'RE TRYING TO ACCOMPLISH AND HOW IT AFFECTS YOU POSITIVELY.

Other ways to say "asset"

"*Dones en acción*" captured the fullest sense of "*asset.*"

The majority of the members at Cristo Rey speak Spanish. The leaders were intrigued by the asset-based approach and wanted to explore it further. But the council at Cristo Rey was wrestling with how to say "asset" in Spanish so that members would understand this approach to congregational life.

First they looked at the Spanish word for "asset" and found that it was too specific to commerce and finance to be applied to the broader meaning they hoped for.

Then they approached some ways of saying "gifts." *Regalos* had a variety of meanings, but council members wondered whether "birthday gift" wouldn't come to most members' minds. *Recursos* wasn't bad, but "resources" usually attached to tangible things, while "asset" should also include qualities and attitudes. *Dones* seemed closer to the idea of "talents" or "gifts from God" but didn't go as far as "asset" did in English.

They soon realized that "gifts" words seemed to stop with the giving or the receiving of gifts. What made "assets" different was that the gifts were put to use.

That sparked Javier's thinking. After a few tries, he came up with a phrase that everyone agreed on: *Dones en acción* captured the fullest sense of "asset." "Gifts in action" indicated that gifts were given (and received) and that those gifts helped build up their congregation.

Dones en acción became the way Cristo Rey began to speak about its new asset-based approach. The congregation readily accepted the idea that they were gifted by God, and that those gifts could be put to use for God's purposes.

ANOTHER LOOK

ASSETS:

POSSESSIONS, TRAITS, EFFECTS, PROPERTY, RESOURCES, VALUED INTANGIBLES, OR WEALTH. FROM THE OLD FRENCH *ASEZ*, ENOUGH (TO SATISFY CREDITORS), PERHAPS ROOTED IN THE VULGAR LATIN *AD SATIS*, TO THE POINT OF SUFFICIENCY.

Chaotic or savvy?

Pastor Marvin didn't need to know about everything and everyone.

Asset-based thinking and planning may seem a little messy—and even chaotic—at first:

❖ People with constant problems or complaints don't get as much attention as they have in the past.

❖ Smaller, newer programs start, and others disappear.

❖ It may be hard to know what's really going on, or who's in charge.

❖ "The plan" may emerge from a sense of vision, either at the start of a group's work or along the way.

Chaotic is how Pastor Marvin felt about asset-based approaches when he first started working in this way. He stuck with the approach, though, and found that over time the difficulties sorted themselves out. The complainers and critics were gradually seeing a new, positive spirit in the congregation. He didn't have to keep propping up ministries that lacked willing or capable leaders. And he grew used to the idea that he didn't need to know about everything and everyone for the congregation to function well.

What made Pastor Marvin and the congregational leaders especially willing to go through a period of chaos? It was their memories of past years when they had to deal with nearly overwhelming incapacity, unwillingness, fatigue and negativity in the congregation.

When all was said and done, Pastor Marvin was willing to put up with what seemed messy about this approach. For the first time in his years of pastoral ministry, he felt that he was a savvy leader, operating with a new kind of wisdom that fit his role as "equipping pastor."

ANOTHER LOOK

BECAUSE THEY ARE NEGATIVE AT THEIR HEART, NEEDS-BASED APPROACHES TO CONGREGATIONAL LIFE EVENTUALLY BECOME NON-SUSTAINABLE AND UNMANAGEABLE. THIS MAY BE A MAJOR FACTOR IN THE BURNOUT OF PASTORS AND OTHER LEADERS.

A way of thinking

At its heart, an asset-based approach is rooted in a different way of thinking about most of life, summarized in these thoughts from Bob, a congregational leader from California:

"I look for positive, useful elements in almost every situation, every person." Bob understands that "positive" doesn't work until "useful" is included. Bob can find good where others may see only problems to be solved.

"I value the relationships God provides me." Relationships with other people are at the heart of Bob's ministry. He has learned to honor, affirm and become excited about other people's assets.

"It helps to name the assets I find in others." Like the ancient Hebrews, Bob understands that when others hear the names of their assets, they begin to know and value themselves better.

"I can live my life satisfied with who I am and what I've been given." The satisfaction that comes from "enough" frees Bob from endlessly seeking "more."

"Asset-based thinking helps me be flexible." Bob takes advantage of changing situations and new assets. (See Case Study 5.)

Asset-based thinking is a way to find excitement and realize hope in what you do. Eventually this kind of thinking can spread into your entire life.

Just ask Bob.

ANOTHER LOOK

THIS KIND OF THINKING ALSO SPREADS INTO THE WAY YOU TREAT YOUR FAMILY, THE DIFFICULTIES YOU FACE, HOW YOU MEASURE YOUR SELF-WORTH, AND HOW YOU LISTEN OR NOTICE "SMALL DETAILS."

A way of planning

When you take an asset-based approach to planning, you begin and end in a place different from the start and finish of "normal" needs-based planning. Listen to the thoughts of Laurel, a congregational stewardship leader from Atlanta:

"I used to think you started planning by listing the needs you wanted to fill." Laurel knows that by the time you put together a plan based on needs, you've weighed yourself down with their sheer volume. Then the thought of all the work they'll need to do in order to solve these problems will weary your fellow planners.

"Now planning takes place in small, quick decisions." As she leads, Laurel can get a group to look at its assets, making decisions about *what to do next together* and acting quickly. She also knows that long-range plans are often modified along the way.

"I've noticed people are more willing to act." As she's used asset-based planning, Laurel has eliminated two major barriers to action in most groups: Their imagined lack of capacity, and the resultant lack of willingness to initiate action.

"When we fulfill our goals, we feel better about trying something else." Laurel knows that success breeds success, and that asset-based planning can sow seeds of creativity, delight and vision.

Laurel has made asset-based planning her preferred way of work. As a congregational leader, she'll never go back to the old, needs-based ways of planning. Laurel has a lot to look forward to.

ANOTHER LOOK

"NEEDS" DON'T DISAPPEAR IN ASSET-BASED PLANNING. THEY'RE JUST NOT THE PLACE TO START, NOR THE PLACE TO GET STUCK. YOU DON'T PLAN IN ORDER TO FILL NEEDS. BUT AS YOU WORK, NEEDS *ARE* FILLED.

The athletic congregation

PASTORS HAVE
ASSETS BEYOND
WHAT'S OBVIOUS.

What would happen if you took advantage of your pastor's athletic abilities? That delightful question faced a suburban Washington congregation a few years ago. The pastors, a clergy couple, gradually answered that question as they joined and formed church sports teams. Because both were accomplished athletes in several sports, they attracted other "athletic types," members and non-members alike. It didn't take long before the congregation attracted new members into its fellowship. After a while, the teams became a reliable outreach method for the congregation.

A CONSISTENT VIEW
OF THE ASSET-BASED
APPROACH IS THAT
IT IS REALLY ALL
ABOUT EVANGELISM.

But there's more. Several of the team members decided to run a children's summer sports camp for kids in the community. As team members became friends, the teams became de facto small groups. A parish hall was refurbished as a gym, ecumenical relationships were begun, and the average age of congregation members trended toward young families. Little by little, sports enthusiasts took up other congregational tasks and became part of the total life of congregational life. What began simply—a couple of pastors enjoying their interest in sports—grew into what the congregation began to call "our sports ministry."

The pastors? They're still athletic, still playing on the teams, and still amazed how the simple asset of athletic ability blossomed into a congregation that knows how to run forward and jump high.

□ MOVEMENT, GROWTH AND CHANGE USUALLY CONTINUE IN AN ASSET-BASED APPROACH, MANY TIMES IN UNEXPECTED WAYS.

□ WHEN COLLECTED OVER TIME, THESE STORIES BECAME PART OF THE CONGREGATION'S IDENTITY.

□ WHAT ADJECTIVE DESCRIBES YOUR CONGREGATION AND HOW IS IT A MINISTRY?

An approach to resources

God doesn't make junk.

Mt. Pisgah Church's leaders wanted to look at their resources in an asset-based way. After a year of working this way, they came up with these principles:

If we have enough of anything, we'll make something out of it. They learned this lesson the day that Charlie, a local cement contractor, wanted to know if the church could use half a load of cement that afternoon. *(George and Stephanie quickly built a form for a new side entrance sidewalk at the home of an elderly member. The cement fit nicely.)*

We'll recycle, re-use or return what we used to waste. They learned this principle the time they almost threw away 10 years' worth of altar candle stubs. *(Frieda knew that the high school art teacher used wax for specific art techniques. The wax candles melted down nicely.)*

Our building is not just for "church." The leaders learned this idea from a nearby congregation that almost closed until it discovered its greatest asset was its building. *(The social ministry team started seeking out small community groups that were just getting started and needed a place to meet. The building worked nicely.)*

God doesn't make junk. They learned this from their mission trip to Mexico. *(Paulo, Al and Gene started collecting and repairing broken bicycles, selling them at garage sales and donating the proceeds to a congregational fund for trade-school scholarships.)*

Now Mt. Pisgah Church has made a promise to God: We will see assets for ministry in everything You give us.

ANOTHER LOOK

CAN YOU FIND THE "ASSETS" IN 100 CANS OF YELLOW HIGHWAY PAINT, A LARGE, GRASSY CHURCHYARD, 36 UNUSED BANNERS, AN OLD SET OF CHURCH DINNERWARE, AND A WEEKLY ANONYMOUS DONATION OF A DOZEN ROSES?

The stewardship dinner

□
**THE PROCESS BEGINS
WITH CAREFUL THINKING,
PROBABLY A VISION
OR YEARNING IN MIND.**

After some thought, the stewardship team at Faith
Church knew that a "stewardship dinner" would be
a good way to gather the congregation together in
fellowship and fun, and a good time to distribute
or collect annual contribution commitments.
They decided to take an asset-based approach.

□
**PERHAPS A GOOD
WAY FOR THE TRULY
COMMITTED TO
BECOME INVOLVED.**

They advertised and invited "whoever was interested
in a stewardship dinner" to come together for
a couple of after-worship planning lunches. Whoever
showed up for these lunches would be the committee.
When the day arrived, about half of the participants
were children and youth. Undeterred, the team went
through a simple asset-mapping process.

□
**LOTS OF INDEX CARDS,
GOOD QUESTIONS
AND BIG TABLES.
(SEE "HOW TO 8:
MAPPING ASSETS.")**

During the mapping process it became apparent
that the majority of this group could do "something
with singing and dancing and acting in it." The first
"Faith Dinner Theater" was born—a combined
dinner, talent festival and stewardship event.

As time went on, the leadership group expanded to double its size, and the talents of about 60 members of the congregation were eventually gathered to make the event a huge success. One wonderful side benefit: children, youth and adults learned to respect each other as they worked together. New friendships were forged, and new appreciation for cross-generational talents and wisdom was evident in other places at Faith.

ONCE THE PROCESS BEGINS, NEW RESOURCES ARE LEVERAGED TOWARD THE VISION OR GOALS.

NOTICE HOW RELATIONSHIPS WERE BUILT BY COMMON PURPOSE AND SHARED WORK.

Beyond "positive thinking"

First assess the realities of both "water" and "glass."

Asset-based approaches move beyond the delightful prospects of "positive thinking." (Positive thinking would stop at the glass being half-full instead of half-empty.) When you use an asset-based approach in your congregation, you first assess the realities of both "water" and "glass," which roots asset-based planning in "what is" before it heads toward "what could be."

Jose-David knows how this works at Todos los Santos, a congregation in a small Minnesota town with Hispanic immigrant workers. Life is hard for his members, at work and in the community. They face long, difficult workdays and the lingering suspicions of townspeople. Their congregation is in the same situation, with seemingly limited resources.

If Jose-David were to start and end his thinking and planning with only positive thinking, his parishioners would dismiss him as unrealistic and out of touch with their lives. He could not function well as their pastor.

While he still maintains a hopeful, forward-looking view of his congregation's vitality, he also approaches planning and thinking with an accurate, even hard-nosed assessment of the assets of this congregation. While he stretches their and his creativity and capacities, he also knows when their and his limits have been reached.

Jose-David believes strongly in his calling as a pastor and in the future of the congregation. That's why he is interested in not only what's good (positive thoughts) but also what's useful (assets).

Jose-David is a positive asset for Todos los Santos congregation.

ANOTHER LOOK

HOW COULD THE CURMUDGEONS AND GAINSAYERS IN YOUR CONGREGATION BE HELPFUL REALISTS IN YOUR ASSET-BASED APPROACHES? HOW ARE THEY HONORED? HOW ARE THEY ENCOURAGED TO BE POSITIVE AS WELL?

Asset-based emotions

You may recognize these emotions.

When you begin working in an asset-based way, expect some feelings to accompany this approach. Some may be new and some familiar, but they're all connected to asset-based thinking and planning. You may recognize these emotions in people who've worked in asset-based approaches for years:

Carolyn, a graduate student: "No matter how busy my life gets, when I think of what God equips me to do, I'm always filled with hope for what lies ahead."

Philip, a leader in a small congregation in the California mountains: "With no pastor, we've come to appreciate each other more—our gifts and not our problems."

Vera, a great-grandmother: "I'm always surprised at what I can still do after all these years."

Paul, who travels a lot: "When I see how Christians everywhere are changing the world around them, I feel like I'm part of something way bigger than just me."

Sheri, a pastor who knows about gratitude: "The people of this church have so much to offer to God's work that it brings tears of joy to my eyes every Sunday."

Julio, a consultant and trainer in asset-based approaches, feels a sense of solidarity among leaders as they find a new way of working together.

Bob, who writes about asset-based thinking: "I'm constantly delighted to meet lots of people who already know this stuff."

ANOTHER LOOK

LIST ALL THE EMOTIONS YOU'VE BEEN FEELING AS YOU'VE READ THIS FIELD BOOK. PUT THEM INTO CATEGORIES LIKE *DESIRABLE* OR *CHALLENGING*. READ ROMANS 12 AGAIN. PRAY ABOUT THE "MIND OF CHRIST" BEING IN YOU.

"Insistence" as asset

☐
ASSET THINKING IS USEFUL AT ANY TIME IN A CONGREGATION'S LIFE CYCLE.

A congregation in the inner core of a mid-sized industrial city in Pennsylvania is near the point of closing. Six other churches lie within a two-mile radius; attendance at worship is fewer than 50 and falling; most members are elderly; only part-time pastoring is affordable; and the endowment is being depleted rapidly. All signs point toward the imminent end of the congregation.

Except for one asset: The congregation's insistence that its well-maintained and centrally located building remain useful.

Members wrestled with what that might mean and they approached other congregations, their denomination's area judicatory officials and community leaders to consider this situation as a new opportunity. Together they've thought about:

❖ a large, combined congregation at multiple sites

❖ a full-service community center at their site

❖ cooperation with gentrifying efforts in the city.

At this point, the efforts haven't yet yielded a new use for the building or a new life for the congregation. But their asset remains the same: a consistent vision that a well-maintained, centrally located and multi-faceted building complex could be useful as a continuing asset for God's purposes in their city.

□ **GOOD WAYS TO THINK SOMETIMES TAKE TIME TO YIELD RESULTS.**

Time will tell whether they are "successful." Time will also tell that their persistence in the face of institutional death WILL BE a lasting legacy of this congregation—an asset for which future generations may thank them.

□ **NOTICE THAT THE CONGREGATION'S THINKING SHIFTED FROM MAINTENANCE TOWARD THE GOOD OF THE WIDER SOCIETY.**

You can do this

Paul approached leaders with a "can-do" attitude.

Imagine eavesdropping on a conversation between St. Paul and the men and women he mentored: Titus, Timothy, Junia, Apollo, Priscilla, Onesimus, Lydia and many others. What would Paul's approach have been to the sizable tasks of gospel proclamation, care and feeding of new Christians, and keeping detractors at bay? Paul approached leaders with a "can-do" attitude.

In the letters to Timothy and Titus, the small anecdotal windows in Acts, and in the endings of his other writings, Paul consistently encouraged leaders who faced daunting tasks. (For starters, read and pray about the letter to Titus.)

Where did Paul get this attitude? Paul derived his approach from an overwhelming sense of being well-equipped for a calling he did not initially choose. He also knew how well God had blessed him and how God constantly encouraged him.

You can find comfort in reading about these early leaders, and specific helps in reading the letters written to them. In fact, you might even think of them as a kind of "first field book" for leaders wanting to take an asset-based approach to this new thing God planted in the world—a church based on free salvation, inspired by the words and actions of Christ Jesus, and commissioned to change the world.

ANOTHER LOOK

A CONGREGATION IN A GAMBLING RESORT TOWN CALLED A PASTOR TO WORK INSIDE THE LARGEST CASINO AS A MINISTRY TO THE WORKERS AND AN ENCOURAGEMENT FOR THE MINISTRIES OF CONGREGATION MEMBERS.

How much bread?

*They tallied
the answers
to Jesus'
question.*

Pastor Holly and the parishioners at Tabernacle Church took seriously Jesus' question to the boy with the lunch: "How much bread do you have? Go and see" (Mark 6). They thought it would be a good question to ask as they began considering establishing a food bank at their church.

So members went home and literally counted loaves of bread in their pantries. The next week they reported the amount. The following week they tallied how much milk they had, then the amount of canned fruits. This kept up, week after week.

At the end of two months the answers to Jesus' question were tallied in a report of total surplus food. Members were astounded to see how many "loaves of bread and fishes" were available for this possible new venture. Thousands of items were available immediately and other foodstuffs were pledged. Some of the strangest answers—20 pots and pans, an exercise bicycle and a never-used set of dishes—suggested answers to questions that would come later.

The decision came easily: We WILL set up a food pantry at Tabernacle because we know how much bread we have. Within weeks "Tabernacle Table" was established, staffed and filled to overflowing with food. In the years since that time, well over 5,000 people have been fed.

ANOTHER LOOK

WHAT WOULD HAPPEN IF YOUR CONGREGATION SUPPLIED ALL THE ITEMS FOR A "KITCHEN UTENSILS NOOK" AT YOUR LOCAL FOOD PANTRY? HOW MUCH DO YOU HAVE? GO AND SEE!

The futility of worry

Jesus' sermon about worry was tough to hear.

The people who listened to Jesus had a lot to worry about: the crushing military might of an occupying army, imminent poverty dogging their every step, injustice all around them, sickness and death a daily occurrence.

That's why Jesus' sermon about worry was tough to hear, and even more difficult to believe—until Jesus added a twist: Worry is futile. "Can you add days to your life by worrying?" Jesus asks. "Don't you have enough to think about today?" (Read and pray about Matthew 6:25-34.)

Even though he railed against the injustices these people endured every day—the Romans, the rich, those who claimed religious authority—Jesus also knew that worry accomplishes nothing. Nothing, that is, except making worriers better capable of worrying more. When it continues, fear-based anxiety becomes a habit that seems to push away most other habits. Maybe even God gets pushed away (see verses 32 and following) and THAT'S an ultimate futility.

How has worry invaded the way your congregation works and thinks? How does it characterize the way you work and think? Can you see how nothing good can come from anxiety, how it changes you into someone you may not like being around? Can you see the complete and utter futility of leading others to uneasiness, disquiet or misgiving?

Good. Now you can listen to what Jesus said about birds and flowers.

ANOTHER LOOK

THE BEST WAY TO STOP WORRYING: COLD TURKEY. BEATING THIS ADDICTION REQUIRES THE SUPPORT OF OTHERS WHO ARE LESS PRONE TO WORRY THAN YOU. HOW WILL YOU ASK THEM FOR HELP?

Power in weakness

Nothing to write home about.

Something was wrong with Paul's body, and he knew it. Some problems with his eyesight, the lingering effects of all those beatings—some kind of "thorn in the flesh." Nothing to write home about.

But Paul could write to the Christians in Corinth that his physical weakness was some kind of asset for his godly work. God's power was strongest when Paul was weak. (Read and pray about 2 Corinthians 12, especially verses 8 and following.)

Where's the asset in "weakness" of any kind? First, it strips from you any idea that you're self-made, self-sufficient or self-perpetuating. When you understand your ultimate weakness, you are relieved of the enormous burden of thinking that you're in charge of everything.

When that happens—to you or to your congregation—
you begin again with dependence on God and on
God's gracious blessings. The blinders of self-idolatry
are gone and you get to see what's *really true:* you have
assets that come from God's abundance. You can
be grateful for even the smallest gift from God.
Now you are powerful.

You may still be weak, of course, but that won't be
who you *really are* when all is said and done. You'll
have come to believe God's power coming through
you and you'll have acted powerfully as well, for the
good of others and to God's glory.

"Powerful in weakness" will be what you write
home about.

ANOTHER LOOK

THE CORINTHIAN
CHURCH WAS A
PROBLEM ALMOST
FROM ITS START.
READ BOTH 1 AND 2
CORINTHIANS TO
UNDERSTAND THIS
"CASE STUDY" OF
ENCOURAGEMENT
FOR A
DYSFUNCTIONAL
CONGREGATION.
AND TAKE HEART...

An asset-rich village

A large village in India seemed to have limited assets by which to move from poverty. What was most visible:

❖ Women who could carry heavy loads

❖ A lot of unused land

But the villagers were not discouraged, especially the women. Starting with those two assets, the village women developed a sense of other assets. These included the large number of women in a new women's cooperative, the government's food-for-work program, and the women's fierce sense that economic justice had been denied them.

The women planned to use those assets together. They excavated dirt to form a large catch basin, and dumped the same dirt around the perimeter to form a large dam. The food-for-work program provided sustenance. The plan made sense. Once the monsoons came (could rain be an asset now?) the dam caught and held the water in the catch basin. Eventually the water percolated into the water table and kept village wells from going dry.

ASSET-BASED COMMUNITY DEVELOPMENT STARTED IN PARTS OF THE WORLD WHERE POVERTY AND INJUSTICE SEEMED OVERWHELMING.

SOME OUTSIDE SOURCES MAY SET UP CO-DEPENDENCIES OR A "WELFARE MENTALITY." HERE THEY ARE USED AS ASSETS.

"FIT" IS WHEN ASSETS WORK TOGETHER, EACH FILLING ITS FUNCTION IN A PLAN THAT JUST MAKES SENSE.

Thus the women and their work ensured ample water for irrigation. The men who were dependent on water for the village orchard were willing to accept the women's cooperative as an economic partner. The social and economic status of the women increased, as did their self-determination.

And the "limited assets"? In a few years no one will remember how women or men could have ever thought that way!

PERHAPS THIS IS THE MOST IMPORTANT ELEMENT IN THE STORY: HOW ATTITUDES WERE CHANGED WHEN ASSET-BASED PLANNING CHANGED BEHAVIORS.

DON'T FORGET: ASSETS ARE RARELY "LIMITED."

SECTION TWO
How To

Using this section

*Put together
your own
sequence
of readings.*

Because *The Great Permission* is a field book, it
includes helps for putting into practice the variety
of ideas you've read about. In the pages that follow,
you'll find materials that:

❖ Help you with specific tasks (see "Mapping assets")

❖ Provide broader "how-to" insight
   (see "Diminishing neediness")

❖ Challenge you to visit new places
   (see "Isolating ideation").

No specific instructions
With few exceptions, the "how to" readings do not
give you step-by-step instructions about what
to do or specific materials you should accumulate.
The asset-based approach is too broad to pin down
to "sure-fire techniques."

Making your own approach

What will make this work for you is to tailor this material for your own situation. Throw out what doesn't apply; keep what fits. Add your own materials. Feel free to skip around as you read. Remember that only you can decide what's useful.

Case studies

Several case studies have been scattered throughout this section. Read the studies and the comments attached to them. How might the situations apply to your congregation and what ideas for action do they suggest?

Taking "Another Look"

Each reading includes these quickly read paragraphs which include questions, comments and suggestions. You might begin your quest here for what to do next.

ANOTHER LOOK

PETER BLOCK, AUTHOR, BUSINESS CONSULTANT AND PHILOSOPHER, SUGGESTS THAT THE BEST ANSWER TO THE QUESTION "HOW?" IS ALWAYS "YES!" SIMPLY STATED, TECHNIQUES SUPPLEMENT THE PRIMARY ASSET—YOUR WILLINGNESS TO RISK ACTION.

Spotting the lively ones

To explore the asset-based approach in your congregation, you'll probably want to find some "lively ones" to work with.

Fran always has a sparkle in her eyes, even after she lost her husband to cancer. She knows what "hope" is all about because she's lived it for so long. Fran is a "lively one."

Stephano and his grandfather Medardo have always "colored outside the lines," and everyone knows how creative they can be. Both are artisans who work with wood. They're quiet but their thoughts are always worth hearing. Stephano and Medardo are "lively ones."

Jeremy loves the fellowship of congregational meals. That's why he always volunteers to organize potluck dinners. Because he thinks ahead and knows how to spot missed details beforehand, Jeremy is a "lively one."

Tammy is a stay-at-home mom who can't take much time away from her children to give to church activities. Still, she's always been able to see the best in other people, and frequently tells them so. Tammy is a "lively one."

These are the kind of people who can make asset-based thinking and planning work well. They're willing to listen to new, hopeful ideas. They think ahead. They have energy and wisdom. They know and love other people.

Start looking for the lively ones; they're going to be your planning/thinking group. They may even end up being your friends!

ANOTHER LOOK

A LARGE CONGREGATION IN SOUTH DAKOTA FINDS MANY OF ITS LIVELY LEADERS AMONG MEMBERS OF ITS SPORTS TEAMS AND SPECIAL-INTEREST GROUPS THAT MEET FOR BREAKFAST.

Finding enterprising leaders

You may find enterprising leaders in congregations with these behaviors:

People who take charge of what interests them. The primary assets of enterprising leaders are their answers to the questions, "What are you good at?", "What do you have that's useful?" and "What do you like to do?" Duty and loyalty are present, but not primary motivators.

Congregations with limited "permission-giving" mechanisms. Enterprising leaders prosper in an atmosphere or structure that is characterized by the lack of multiple gatekeepers, invisible permission-givers, micro-managers or lengthy decision-making processes.

Leaders who are continually equipped. Asset-based congregations provide training for leaders, frequent opportunities for learning from each other, and designated times for spiritual growth.

Ability to end programs or ministries. Asset-based planning is realistic. If you don't have the assets to sustain a program or ministry, close it down. (The courage to do this is also an asset!)

Varied ways to find leaders. Electing leaders is only one way to find them. Leadership bubbles up best from simple and continued conversations about faith and life.

Accountability beyond shame and blame. Enterprising leaders take risks and learn from their failures. Their method—talking with peers about what they're doing and receiving feedback.

ANOTHER LOOK

A CONGREGATION IN DETROIT USES PART OF EVERY COUNCIL MEETING AS A TIME FOR BIBLE STUDY AND FAITH SHARING. THE COUNCIL PRESIDENT THINKS THE TIME IS WELL USED BECAUSE IT DEVELOPS LEADERS AND SETS A TONE.

Equipping the saints

At its heart, an asset-based approach to congregational life supports the radical proposition that God uses the church to equip the saints for their ministries in the world. (Read and pray about Ephesians 4:11-12 or 2 Timothy 3:17.)

The elders at Christ Church know how that works because their mission statement already includes that language.

Mike became a pastor after a career in a caring profession NOT because he wanted to be a better caregiver, but because he wanted people to develop their own assets to care for others.

Enrique and Isabel, now in their 80s, know that their whole life—and this congregation—is a legacy that will influence the godly lives of generations coming up behind them.

Ellie Mae works tirelessly for the congregation, not only because she loves being with the people of Christ Church on Sundays, but also because she knows what these people do in their daily stewardship Monday through Saturday.

Fred is a bus driver who sees driving as his "life mission." His congregation's shared wisdom helped him turn days of drudgery into small, exciting conversations with people who need a lift.

Each of these leaders sees Christ Church as more than an organization requiring its members' energy, time and money. What they see is "an equipping place" and the good that comes to all members because of their leadership.

ANOTHER LOOK

DAILY LIFE STEWARDSHIP IS ONE WAY TO TALK ABOUT HOW YOU WORK AT FULFILLING GOD'S WILL FOR THE ENTIRE WORLD. YOU DECIDE WHAT TO WORK ON, COLLECT YOUR ASSETS AND THEN GET TO WORK ALONGSIDE OTHER STEWARDS.

Energizing "inactives"

You probably already know who they are, these "inactives." They're people like Stanley, and they may seem like a problem to most congregations.

Stanley is a single parent whose children are in high school. He's coming to the end of his "soccer dad" career, but still doesn't have much use for the church since his wife divorced him. It's not that the church treated him poorly, but Stanley feels just a little ashamed or even embarrassed to come to worship often. It seems easier to stay on the sidelines.

But if you talked to Stanley, you'd find out that he still carries inside some deep spiritual questions. At work, he's responsible for a lot of money and quite a few people, and he tries to make ethical, even godly decisions. He's talented in a number of ways, and has more free time now that his two boys are about ready to graduate.

Stanley could be energized by this asset-based approach because it's something unique and challenging—and because it matches some of the approaches he's been learning to use at work. Stanley could even get excited.

All he needs is your invitation to become part of an asset-based planning team. All he wants is to be known for what he's good at, not for the mistakes he's made in the past. All he knows is that he's really not "inactive" in his faith at all. Stanley could energize your asset-based team into an exciting, front-edge ministry.

ANOTHER LOOK

AN ESTABLISHED CONGREGATION ON THE WEST COAST FOUND THAT MANY INACTIVE MEMBERS WERE EMPTY NESTERS. THE CONGREGATIONAL LEADERS SUSPECT THAT THERE'S AN ASSET SOMEWHERE IN THE IDEA OF "INACTIVES."

Energizing neighbors

One of the most important assets of St. James' Church is its neighborhood; more precisely, the asset of the people who live in the area served by the congregation. St. James' neighbors—even those who are "unchurched"—are energized by the prospect that they, too, can be valuable partners in the ministry of this small-but-lively congregation.

Members of the congregation have always made it a point to know their locale not only for its needs, but also for its rich possibilities. Skills, experience, relationships are found in abundance in the streets and hallways of the neighborhood, in the homes and work places around the church. Friendships, favors-to-be-returned, community pride, and mutual respect all come to St. James' programs from the people outside the congregation. Members of the community are willing to reciprocate, to give when asked, to pitch in and partner with St. James.

Why? St. James' members have affirmed "non-members" as more than needy, have found excellence in the nooks and crannies of people's lives, and have been hospitable to their neighbors in a hundred small ways. The neighbors see Jesus Christ in the love and respect they receive from St. James. Some neighbors have come to accept Christ as their Savior, and to make St. James a part of their life more fully. Sometimes the neighbors initiate ideas for programs or events!

St. James' neighbors realize that they will always be an asset for the congregation, just as they hope that its ministries will continue to hold great value for them.

ANOTHER LOOK

HOW DO YOU DEFINE "MEMBER" AND "NONMEMBER"? HOW WELL DO BOTH GROUPS KNOW EACH OTHER? AND JUST WHO ARE YOUR NEIGHBORS?

Explaining "assets"

When you start asset-based thinking and planning, you're eventually going to get a big "HUH?" about the word asset. It's not that hard to explain; it just depends on how you think of yourself.

Think of yourself as a teacher with class notes. Photocopy the reading, "'Acid' in our church?" (page 12) or any other reading in this book, and hand it out every time you get a similar question.

Think of yourself as a historian. Think of other places where some good concept or skill in the Christian church came from outside the church. Just like "asset," these ideas originated in the world.

Think of yourself as a storyteller. Tell a story about how a seemingly useless "gift" (or one that was never used) turned into an asset when it was put into use. (See Case Study 4.)

Think of yourself as a bulletin board artist.
Make a bulletin board at church with the word
ASSET right in the middle. Print out synonyms on
pieces of paper, and join them by yarn to *ASSET*.
(See the reading, "Other ways to say 'asset'",
page 34.) Invite viewers to add their own ideas.

**Think of yourself as a philosopher with good
questions.** Reply to questioners with any one of these
questions: "What do you have that's useful?", "What
are you good at doing?" and "What do you like to do?"
The answers of the questioner are their assets.

Another Look

A LOVING MOTHER
SEWED BATHING
SUITS FOR HER
SONS. THE BOYS'
REACTION: "THE
OTHER KIDS WILL
LAUGH AT THE
LITTLE WHALES
ON OUR TRUNKS!"
THE BATHING
SUITS WERE
GIFTS—THEY WERE
GIVEN AND
RECEIVED—BUT
WERE NOT ASSETS.
THEY WERE
NEVER WORN.

The event-based congregation

SETTING AND CONTEXT
ARE IMPORTANT ASSETS.

A very small congregation in rural Oregon approached youth ministry with a single asset in mind: the pastor and members both liked camping trips. Their logic was simple and profound:

1. We're good at organizing several-day camping trips with family and friends.

2. We could include the few teens in our congregation.

NOTICE WHOM ELSE THE
ASSET BENEFITS.

3. These teens may want to invite friends.

4. We'll talk and work together on these trips; we'll get to know each other well. This could be the start of "relational ministry!"

So they began with a once-a-year fishing trip, led by

IN ASSET-BASED
THINKING PEOPLE ARE
NOTICED AND HONORED
FOR THE BEST IN
THEMSELVES. "SKILLED"
AND "EXPERIENCED"
ARE GOOD WAYS TO
CHARACTERIZE ASSETS.

skilled and experienced outdoors types. The conversations were deep, personal and exquisitely spiritual. The minds and bodies of adults and teens were refreshed. The fishing was very good.

Within a few years, the congregation began to realize
that these events could be the basis for other areas
of typical congregational programming. They began
to think about family camps, festivals and community
events. New relationships, new members, and new
connections—all made possible because of the assets
of events. A sustainable, exciting and manageable
way of doing church was born.

□ **ASSET-BASED
APPROACHES
USUALLY INCLUDE
SIDE BENEFITS.**

□ **WHAT'S
"SUSTAINABLE"
IS ALSO USUALLY
"MANAGEABLE."**

Planning your work

As you begin planning in an asset-based way, use this quick description as a guide for your work.

Exploration
Like first-time explorers, asset-based planners look broadly and deeply together at directions, goals and possibilities. They come to agreement about a general purpose or outcome.

Asset mapping
Participants collect and organize individual and group assets into a coherent, visible map of their collected capabilities. Order and direction emerge out of what at first seems chaotic.

Relationship building
Positive, hopeful and productive relationships are forged when participants reveal their capabilities, their willingness to explore their hopes, and their success in working with others.

Gathering the community

Asset-based planning honors and includes all who
have an interest or stake in a particular aspect of
congregational life. "All" can include some amazing
people, including children. (See Case Study 3.)

Leveraging resources

Participants in asset-based planning discover,
dislodge, develop and disseminate the resources
of a group of people. Resources (assets) are used
efficiently and in effective combinations. The assets
of the wider community are included.

ANOTHER LOOK

A CONGREGATION
IN OHIO WAS
AMAZED TO FIND
YOUTH, ADULTS
AND CHILDREN
WHO HAD AN
INTEREST IN
MUSICAL DRAMA.
WITHIN A FEW
MONTHS, THEY
FOUND, PRACTICED
AND OFFERED
A DELIGHTFUL
STEWARDSHIP
MUSICAL.

Mapping assets

One of the most important steps in asset-based planning is the task of asset mapping. Follow this simple outline to gather your group's assets together in a helpful way.

1. Start with people who are motivated for the task you have in mind.

2. Come together in a place where you can spread out—where walls, tables or floor provide plenty of space.

3. Characterize the task you have in mind and answer questions about its general scope. (Note: You may map the group's assets with or without a specific outcome in mind. This process works for groups who are clear about their mission before they begin, as well as for those who want the map to give them direction.)

4. Distribute markers and slips of paper or index cards, as many as 25–30 per participant.

5. Ask the participants to list assets, one per card, that might be useful in undertaking the task you have chosen. Ask these questions:
   - What do you have that's useful?
   - What are you good at doing?
   - What do you like to do?

6. Construct a "map" of the assets by laying all the slips of paper or cards where all can see them.
   - Invite participants to link the assets into logical categories. Some folks call this "clumping" or "connecting." (See "Learning from the map," page 86.)

7. Look at the categories to see how your group's concentrations of assets connect to accomplish an action. Talk about what you see.

8. From your strengths (your assets) decide what to do next, who will do what, and when the tasks will be completed. Then vote with your feet and start walking together.

BRAIN SCIENTISTS DESCRIBE "MAP-MAKING" AS ONE OF THE BRAIN'S FAVORITE ACTIVITIES AND A METAPHOR FOR MOST LEARNING PROCESSES. MAPPING IS A "WHOLE-BRAIN" ACTIVITY, WHICH IS WHY ASSET MAPPING OFFERS THE SAME POSSIBILITIES AND PLEASURES.

85

Learning from the map

"The map tells you what to do next." That sentence describes what Terry experiences every time he leads a group through asset mapping. People start sifting and grouping assets into categories. Suddenly an "aha" moment occurs: someone notices how assets fit together and how they point in an obvious direction. Each time it happens, Terry remembers that people are really pretty good at discovering what to do next. He's learned to wait for that moment to occur.

Follow these steps to help people "learn from the map:"

1. Physically clump the asset-bearing cards together for easy viewing.

2. Look at the map, looking for relationships:
   - cause and effect
   - logical sequence (what's first, what's next)
   - size or strength of categories
   - similarities and differences
   - what allows or supports what

- relative ease of effort
- what repeats itself
- whose assets appear in what categories

3. Move the asset-bearing cards around to see and think about alternate ways of combining assets.

4. Ask this question: "If this is what we have, what we are good at, and what we like to do, what does the map tell us about what to do next?"

5. Although you're thinking only about what to do next, don't be surprised if someone comes up with a grander vision.

Tape or otherwise fasten together the clumps of the map so that you can use it again at another time.

ANOTHER LOOK

A SMALL CHICAGO CONGREGATION ASKED MEMBERS TO COMPLETE ASSET CARDS AS AN OFFERING. THE NEXT SUNDAY THEIR ASSET MAP WAS HUNG IN THE ENTRYWAY. NOW WORSHIPERS REMEMBER THEIR GOD-GIVEN CAPABILITIES. THIS WAY THEY'RE RARELY DISCOURAGED.

Avoiding relapses

The stewardship team at Peace Church was worried. Although they'd had a pleasant experience using asset mapping to plan a successful fall stewardship program, they sensed that other leaders were falling back into familiar patterns—first thinking about needs. The team members knew that if they could avoid relapses, asset-based thinking could be helpful for a long time.

They decided to re-use the map they had first constructed for the stewardship program, with some variations:

❖ One member entered the assets into a data base program for easy retrieval during the rest of the year.

❖ Another team member tidied up the map by transferring it to colored construction paper. She re-taped the new map and hung it in the fellowship room. The title read, "One Set of Assets at Peace Church. Others Will Emerge."

❖ A third member of the team took the original map and asked that it be included as part of the congregation's annual "Blessing of Gifts" Sunday. He wrote a prayer about the map, and gave it to the worship team as a model for its own prayer times.

❖ The leader of the team brought the now well-worn map to every council meeting and explained pieces of it as part of her report each meeting, until after six months the whole map had been thoroughly reviewed.

Over a few months, members and leaders of the congregation saw the map many times. They started imagining how asset maps that included them might look. Soon relapses were not a problem.

How are relapses a problem and an opportunity? How could relapses encourage change? How could you prepare for these returns to the former behaviors? What would you pray about?

ANOTHER LOOK

COUNCIL MEMBERS IN A SOUTH CAROLINA CONGREGATION KEEP TRACK OF BUSINESS MANAGEMENT TRENDS BY SHARING BOOKS AND ARTICLES. THIS HELPS THEM AVOID RELAPSES.

Naming assets

It's possible that as you enter an asset-based way of thinking and planning you might not know all the kinds of assets that exist. Here are some questions to help you name as "extraordinary" assets what others might see as "ordinary."

Who do you know well? In our culture, especially in well-established communities, this matter lies at the heart of many decisions.

Who owes you a favor? Social favors can be important assets, especially when you want to gather together assets from outside your congregation.

What did you used to be good at doing? Most of your skills don't go away; they just get rusty. Asset-based thinking can sharpen and polish supposedly lost excellence.

What do you have a lot of? Excess food, items, participants or skill means that some of it could be wasted or ignored. An asset-based approach doesn't let that happen.

What's invisibly good about this congregation?
Positive attitudes, a long history, and community
respect—these seemingly invisible attributes are
also strong assets for any actions you might want
to take together.

What's "just so crazy it might work?" Sometimes
the least likely skill, experience or possession can
spark an entire change in direction or program.

As you answer any of these questions, you'll be adding
to your knowledge about the resources and gifts God
has given you. All of them will become assets once
you put them to use, for God's good purposes.

ANOTHER LOOK

A NEW
CONGREGATION
IN TEXAS BEGAN
MEETING IN
A FORMER
FUNERAL PARLOR.
THAT UNLIKELY
LOCATION WAS
AN ASSET: THE
PROPERTY WAS
INEXPENSIVE AND
MOST PEOPLE
IN TOWN ALREADY
KNEW THE
NEW CHURCH'S
LOCATION!

Building capabilities

One of the delightful surprises about the asset-based approach is how it can add to your abilities. Amazingly, when people talk together about what they are good at doing, what they have that's good or what they like to do—they encounter a kind of "multiplier effect."

The people at St. Andrews know how that works. They began their work on a new family ministry by naming assets out loud. After a few minutes of conversation, Vera spoke about her many years of preparing a family history. Without any prompts, Malik, Frieda and Marcus suddenly remembered their own interest in reading about families. *One person's assets triggered others' recall.*

Phil sat through most of the conversation without saying much. Finally, when someone asked, he explained that he was quiet because he was drawn towards his deepest, oldest and most positive feelings about himself. *Asset naming invites deep discovery.*

Without waiting to be asked, the others started listing what they believed were Phil's useful personal attributes for this ministry. Their assessment of Phil was accurate and the list quickly grew longer. *Asset-based approaches provide opportunities for appreciation and affirmation.*

When the meeting was over, Vera, Malik, Frieda, Marcus and Phil left with a feeling of new respect and admiration for each other and a willingness to take the next steps. *Asset naming builds love, trust and respect in a group.*

As you engage in asset-based approaches, be ready for your assets to multiply. And be amazed at God's ability to make that happen.

ANOTHER LOOK

SOME QUESTIONS YOU MAY USE TO MULTIPLY ASSETS: DOES ANYBODY ELSE HAVE THE SAME ASSET? WHAT DOES THIS ASSET REMIND YOU OF ABOUT YOURSELF? WHAT ASSETS DO YOU SEE IN OTHER PEOPLE?

Diminishing neediness

Dorothy, a laid-off technology worker, understands that she doesn't deserve anything God provides, that she's "needy" before God. Because she's been out of work for a while, it's hard to think of anything except what she's missing or lacking in life. That attitude had motivated her necessary repentance and seeking of God's favor. But Dorothy wondered, "What motivates the rest of my life as a Christian?" Is "needy" the best description of the fullness that God creates in her?

It took a few meetings with the planning group at St. Germaine to persuade Dorothy that "presumed neediness" was robbing her of her willingness to do much more than accept sympathy. The group was taking an asset-based approach to build a playground for the neighborhood, and they asked Dorothy to be part of the team. As soon as Dorothy started talking about "what we need to get this job done," the group stopped her. They said they wanted her first to think about what she could contribute to the project from her personal skills and experience.

Suddenly it hit her: the more she made decisions out of a position of neediness, the less she had to contribute and the more she subtracted from the group's capabilities. What had to happen instead? Dorothy realized that she could become aware of what gifts God had given her, and this group would help. On that day, Dorothy's neediness started to diminish.

ANOTHER LOOK

"PRESUMED NEEDINESS" BECOMES A HABIT BECAUSE YOUR BRAIN GETS USED TO FINDING "WHAT'S WRONG" AS ITS NORMAL WAY OF THINKING. A SMALL BRAIN PATHWAY GRADUALLY TURNS INTO A COMMUTER HIGHWAY.

Praying past needs

Overactive neediness had worked its way into the prayer life of Salem Church. Well-meaning members had turned times of prayer into an increasingly sad recitation of the woes and worries of the congregation. At worship or in groups they prayed for "all people according to their needs" almost exclusively. For years they had completely overlooked the balanced approach suggested in their worship book: pray for the "whole people of God."

Latesha, a high school honor student and track star, noticed the problem, and talked to her mother. "Aren't we supposed to thank God for what's good, too?" she asked. Her mother talked to a few friends, but they had no suggestions for changing the situation.

On the way home from a track meet one Saturday, Latesha, her mom and two of Latesha's friends started talking about what they could request as subjects for the next Sunday's prayers. They would ask the prayer leader to thank God for the graduating seniors and for a week of much-needed rain. The next Sunday they would request the pastor to pray on behalf of all the medical personnel who attend Salem and thank God for their service on God's behalf.

It took about two months before other members joined in, adding petitions of thankfulness and blessing. A year later the prayer life of the congregation had moved beyond listing needs in worship, meetings or small groups. Salem had learned to pray past needs.

ANOTHER LOOK

WHAT WOULD HAPPEN IF YOU MET WITH WORSHIP LEADERS AND LOOKED FOR PLACES IN WHICH "GOD'S ABUNDANCE" SHOWS UP IN PRAYERS, HYMNS, CHILDREN'S MESSAGES AND SERMONS? WHAT WOULD CHANGE?

Auditing and editing

Diminishing the sometimes-overwhelming presence of needs-based thinking in a congregation may be as simple as auditing and editing the verbal and written messages you send and receive. Here's what might happen if you brought together an "auditing and editing" group once a year.

Auditing starts with counting. First, go through congregational communications—mailings, reports, newsletters, even copies of sermons—tallying words like "need," "just," "only" and negative adjectives and adverbs.

Auditing includes balancing. Now go back through the same communications and look for positive words or phrases that balance out negativity.

Editing means excising. Next take your editing pens and cross out every instance of "needy" language.

Editing means rewriting. Go to the authors of the original communication and suggest changes that would be more positive and encouraging.

Auditing looks at the big picture. Write a report to the church council about what you've found, especially the positive changes you've seen in writers. This way, you add positive reinforcement as a way of motivating and encouraging long-term change.

This process could be fun! By your example, you could gradually help change the entire tone of communications in the congregation. And after that, who knows what might happen!

ANOTHER LOOK

SOME PLACES
YOU MIGHT LOOK
FOR NEEDS-HEAVY
COMMUNICATION
IN YOUR
CONGREGATION:
FINANCIAL
REPORTS,
THE WORK
OF NOMINATING
COMMITTEES,
SERMONS ON
STEWARDSHIP,
AND MAILINGS
TO ALL MEMBERS.

Assessing before evaluating

You can understand asset-based planning a little bit better if you know something about gold and silver mining in the mid-to-late-1800s in the Western United States.

Prospectors dig and poke around dirt and rocks. Asset-prospectors dig among the most ordinary places in a congregation's life, looking for something valuable.

Prospectors know how to see gold where others see only rocks. Asset prospectors can find useful assets hiding inside ordinary people.

Prospectors can't be tricked by "fools' gold." Asset-prospectors are realists, knowing the difference between "assets" and scant "positive thinking."

Prospectors take promising ore to an assayer. Asset-based planners ask for the group's help in deciding the worth of the assets they uncovered.

Prospectors stake claims and mine the ore. Asset-prospectors work hard to extract extensive worth from the "ore" of the gifts they have unearthed in the congregation.

Prospectors take the ore somewhere to be refined into pure metals. Asset-prospectors help improve the gifts they find in people. Strangely, these assets multiply in the process.

Prospectors don't get into arguments about "their rights" and "their claim." Asset-planners understand that all claims of ownership start with God.

ANOTHER LOOK

LIKE MINERS, ASSET-PROSPECTORS ARE PLUCKY, HAVE GOOD TOOLS, WORK HARD, ARE NOT AFRAID OF THE DARK, GET EXCITED EASILY, HAVE GOOD EYESIGHT, ARE ALWAYS HOPEFUL AND SO NEVER RUN OUT OF ENERGY.

Counteracting presumed neediness

The story is told of a helpful Boy Scout who spies what appears to be a helpless elderly woman waiting to cross the street. Without regard for his safety, the scout darts through heavy traffic, grabs the arm of the woman and escorts her across the street. It is only when the woman's bus passes by—now on the opposite side of the street—that the scout realizes the mistake of presuming neediness when none existed. The elderly woman learned the lesson years ago.

You can counter your own urge for too-quick helpfulness in some simple ways:

If you don't know, don't imagine neediness first. Keep your helpfulness focused only on the places where you know need exists, and where your help will be valuable.

Don't mistake your desire for change as someone else's need. "The youth in this church need to learn more about serving others" may be true existentially. But it may more accurately name your yearning for their best interest.

Ask good questions. "May I help you?" is a good question if you accept "No" for an answer. "What's it like to be a (name the person's occupation) these days?" is a neutral question. "What's ahead for you this week?" works well on the way out of worship.

Look for what's good in a person. Even the most vexed or troubled person possesses admirable traits and capabilities. Talk about these matters when you characterize the person to others, or when you talk to him or her.

ANOTHER LOOK

YOU CAN SHOW LOVE AND CARING WITH THESE NON-NEEDY QUESTIONS: WHAT ARE YOU LOOKING FORWARD TO TODAY? WHAT'S GOING WELL FOR YOU THESE DAYS? WHAT HAVE YOU JUST FINISHED? WHAT ARE YOU WORKING ON?

When assets are not

The "new ideas" team in a suburban church in Indianapolis thought they would use the asset-based approach to "find more people to help our pastor with his visits." The first discussion was about the problems they were experiencing:

☐ **BUT RESPONSIBILITY STILL REMAINS WITH THE PASTOR.**

☐ **A "PROBLEM-SOLVING" APPROACH MAY STILL BE NEEDS BASED AND NOT FOCUSED ON ASSETS.**

* People waiting too long for home visits by the pastor.

* Emergency visits taking priority over all other visits.

* The congregation's membership growth overwhelming the visitation program's capabilities.

Next they agreed how many people would be needed to help the pastor. Then they made a list of the members in the congregation they were pretty sure were good at visiting people. Their anticipated next tasks included:

☐ **THIS SEEMS A RATHER FEEBLE ATTEMPT AT FINDING ASSETS.**

☐ **A BETTER APPROACH: PERSONAL INVITATION.**

* Phoning the list of likely visitors to ask if they would be willing to help the pastor.

- Making a three-year plan of how to increase the size of this program.

- Asking their denomination for resources or other help in knowing how to train visitors.

> **TOO FAR AHEAD; CONDITIONS WILL CHANGE.**

Within a few months, the "visitation program" went sour. Most of the likely visitors were already over-committed in the congregation. The three-year plan fizzled when the group disagreed about how much money it would require. The denominational office suggested that the team "probably already knows how to visit people."

> **ASKING "EXPERTS" ABOUT HOW TO DO SOMETHING CAN HIDE YOUR OWN CAPABILITIES AND DELAY ACTION.**

The pastor still makes all the visits; he is now about two years behind.

Avoiding cliques

As a leader, you want to know where your congregation's informal power centers are—those small groups of long-time members who shape the congregation's culture, feed key information to each other, and influence decisions behind closed doors. Since these groups can easily exclude others and taint the spirit of the congregation, they are rarely considered an asset.

At Old Northbrook Church, Pastor Gwynne avoided this problem and honored the assets of this group's power. How?

❖ She is secure in the dimensions of her own personal power and doesn't consider this group a threat.

❖ She views them as "wise elders" and not competition.

❖ She respects these leaders' sense of history that motivates them to protect and build up the legacy of this centuries-old congregation.

❖ She takes time to get to know each member individually, realizing that they are well known, well loved and well connected to the community.

❖ She honors them for having kept the congregation going during a time of difficult transition.

What keeps this group from becoming a usual church clique? The members remain constructive and helpful. They engage others outside the group in their conversations; they include others in their decision-making. They exemplify the hopeful, forward-looking spirit of this congregation that has persisted over many generations.

Is it possible for a congregation to have power groups that don't develop into cliques? Yes, and when it happens, that's an asset.

ANOTHER LOOK

IF POWER IS OFTEN LADEN WITH NEGATIVE EMOTIONS, THEN POWER GROUPS (YOUR CONGREGATION IS FULL OF THEM) CAN RARELY BE AN ASSET. HOW CAN YOU VIEW POWER POSITIVELY?

Curing complainers

Pastor Carolyn decided to put her family systems training into practice. She's been pastor at Faith for two years and it's time to "cure" a clutch of comfortable complainers. She will start with her own personal assets and add the advice of two trusted council members. Here is her plan:

1. **Talk to the five core complainers.** She will meet them in their homes and talk about the specific effects of their continuing negativity.

2. **Assert her new control of the situation.** She will tell them that she won't be available any more to listen to or deal with their negative comments.

3. **Offer them limited choices for their behavior.** They can either contribute to the well-being of the congregation or not take part in what seems to be detrimental to their own well-being.

ANOTHER LOOK

4. **List their (hidden?) assets.** If she senses some latent passions, Pastor Carolyn will talk with them about their personal assets for faithful stewardship of God's plan.

5. **Come to the congregation council if the behavior persists.** Her ministry is to the whole congregation and to assist all members in their ministries. The council can either take charge of the situation or risk seeing Pastor Carolyn devoting her time to a few members' negativity.

Pastor Carolyn is nervous but still looking forward to putting the plan into action. She sees this situation as a test of whether or not an asset-based approach will characterize the congregation from now on.

This will be a watershed time in her life.

DURING THE LATTER YEARS OF HIS LIFE, JEWISH RABBI AND FAMILY SYSTEMS EXPERT EDWIN FRIEDMAN WENT SO FAR AS TO SUGGEST THAT PERPETUALLY COMPLAINING MEMBERS SHOULD BE GIVEN ONLY THE CHOICES OF CHANGING THEIR BEHAVIOR OR LEAVING.

Isolating ideation

ideation, n. (eye-dee-AY-shun) The process of making any action, perceived good or possibility into an idea or ideal. When prolonged, can delay decision-making.

If you're going to make this asset-based approach work, you may want to find a way to "isolate ideation." That means keeping discussion to a minimum and so retaining energy and enthusiasm for actually doing something about the idea. Here's how:

Avoid endless discussion. Discussion can stop at ideas and ideals, and may be only "about something" and not "about us."

Stay away from endlessly "defining terms." Although it helps to agree on what you mean, mutual crafting of definitions keeps emotion-sharing and action to a minimum.

Move toward decisions for action. A frequent indictment of groups locked in needs-based thinking is this: "When all is said and done, much is said and nothing's done."

Ask different questions and look for different answers. Ask questions about personal reactions to ideas as well as questions about feelings or possible decisions that flow from the ideas or ideals.

Beware of "staying on the subject." It's important to remember that conversations are the roots for change, and that conversations rarely stay focused for very long on a single idea.

Remember the value of "good ideas." Probably about a dime a dozen, but an idea that is well acted-upon is a rare and cherished treasure.

ANOTHER LOOK

A FORMER MEAT WORKER CUTS TO THE CHASE WITH A SIMPLE QUESTION: WHAT DO WE WANT TO DO ABOUT THIS IDEA? THE ANSWERS USUALLY LEAD TO DECISIONS FULL OF WILLING ACTION.

Giving thanks 1

A mother teaches her young children to begin their bedtime prayers: "Dear God, thank you for today...." She understands a simple fact: one way to approach life with an asset-based lens is to make "thanks-giving" your preferred behavior. In this way, you'll act your way into thinking in an asset-based way. Here are some simple ways to soak your life with visible gratitude.

Thank people for tasks, behavior or attitudes that might easily be overlooked. Another way to think about this: look behind the scenes.

Keep a supply of stamped thank-you cards by your telephone or at work.

Discipline yourself to include "thanks" as part of most daily conversations.

Select one person who has greatly shaped your life— a teacher, mentor, coach, pastor, friend—and at Christmas card time thank her or him for influencing your life. Be specific.

Thank service personnel for their work or attitudes. Food servers, janitors, clerks, cashiers—each of these people deserves your gratitude for their part in making society function smoothly.

Surprise your pastor with your gratitude about something other than "the nice sermon."

Pray for a discerning spirit and a glad heart. Then begin to name your daily blessings.

The important element in all of these behaviors is consistent and continuing practice. Ask a trusted friend to watch for your relapses into negativity or forgetfulness about gratitude. You can look forward to this way of living!

ANOTHER LOOK

A SUBURBAN CHICAGO CONGREGATION REPLACED "CARE REQUESTS" WITH GRATITUDE POST CARDS. WORSHIPERS ARE INVITED TO WRITE A THANK-YOU NOTE TO ANY CONGREGATION MEMBER, PLACING THE NOTE IN THE OFFERING PLATE. THE OFFICE STAFF MAILS THE CARDS.

Giving thanks 2

"Thank you" was starting to wear thin for members of Good Shepherd. For years they had been a "thanks-giving and thanks-living" congregation, but somehow the emotions and power of gratitude had become thin from overuse.

Samantha, the leader of the youth group, had an idea that she had learned in a youth leadership course. It was simple: Connect "thank you" to the mission of the organization. The congregation leaders agreed to try the idea.

Edgar revised the copy on "donor thank you notes" (quarterly giving statements) so that they all started with the phrase, "Because of you..." and included a story about what had been accomplished because of donor generosity.

Felipe asked the worship team to insert "mission mindedness" into the prayers at worship, so that simple "thanks" became thanks for the part of God's mission the congregation had accepted or was working on.

Sara got excited about devoting a continuing bulletin board to "thanks to you" notes and cards received from institutions and godly enterprises the congregation supported. Mission would be implicit in every thank you that was posted.

Pastor Edmund inspired the stewardship team with a different way of making visits to seek commitments. "Mission conversations" connected members' contributions with the good that was accomplished and with their personal privilege to carry out God's mission in their daily lives.

Good Shepherd is still a "thanks-giving and thanks-living congregation," but now "thanks for God's mission among us" has been added.

ANOTHER LOOK

LOOK FOR "MISSION" IN CONVERSATIONS, THE WAYS IN WHICH MONEY IS SPENT, AND THE SPOKEN YEARNINGS OR PASSIONS OF LEADERS. A GOOD QUESTION TO START MISSION (OR STEWARDSHIP) THINKING: WHY DO YOU HAVE WHAT YOU HAVE?

Fostering generosity

A small group at Living Waters Church wanted to use an asset-based approach to help increase the congregation's sense of generosity. They came up with these ideas and committed themselves to these actions.

Every time we list assets, we will display the results. The group realized that visible evidence of assets— attached to specific individuals—was a good way of remembering their capabilities. They found three new spaces for bulletin boards, and asked the church council to post the assets for every decision they made.

We will thank people for their generosity of spirit, time and money. The group fanned out among congregation members for two months, making it a point to notice every instance of generosity and to personally thank individuals.

We will talk together about how we learned generosity. For five meetings in a row the group talked at length about their formative experiences of self-giving. They studied Bible stories and prayed for this attitude to continue in their lives.

We will talk with others about our experiences with scarcity and abundance. Some group members still remembered times of wealth or poverty in their lives and volunteered to share those experiences with the entire group. (Later, a stewardship sermon grew out of those conversations.)

We will commit to increasing our financial contributions. Because they know that generous hearts show themselves in generous actions, they committed to increased percentages of contributions to Living Waters and the wider church.

ANOTHER LOOK

TRY THESE
GENEROSITY
QUESTIONS:
WHAT DO YOU
DO WITH ASSETS
LEFTOVER FROM
A PROJECT
OR MINISTRY?
WHERE ELSE IN
LIFE DO YOU KEEP
"GIVING IT AWAY"?
WHAT ASSETS
DO YOU NEVER
RUN SHORT OF?

The turned-around "problem"

Denominational stewardship officials had a problem:
A promising program of Hispanic stewardship was
running into a wall called *limosna*. The wall was easy
to describe. Hispanic Christians were consistently
generous with their money and time when faced
with the misfortunes and despair of others. Their
alms giving (*limosna*) was immediate but it was also
short-lived. It created problems for the long-term
funding of congregational ministries.

**How is describing
problems in precise
language not
an asset?**

For months the Hispanic and Anglo officials
worked together to solve this "problem" until one
day two asset-based questions occurred to them:
What if we thought of this problem as an asset?
What would we do with it then?

**When answered,
these two questions
can turn around
almost any problem.**

The answers came tumbling out: We would name this
kind of solidarity and generosity as a good thing. We
would encourage Hispanic Christians to sustain *limosna*
over a longer period of time. We would connect this
kind of immediately reactive generosity with the love

**"Connecting" is
more like "cementing
together."**

Hispanics show towards their families over long periods of time. We would name the church as a real family. We would teach others about this idea.

Within a short period of time, what had been a problem became the cornerstone for an entire program of Hispanic stewardship called *Los regalos de Dios* (The Gifts of God).

The "wall" remained standing because it was an asset. The problem became its own solution.

WHEN YOU TEACH SOMETHING, YOU BELIEVE IT MORE STRONGLY, KNOW IT MORE SURELY AND PRACTICE IT MORE EFFECTIVELY.

YOU DON'T HAVE TO BULLDOZE PROBLEMS TO SOLVE THEM.

Developing leaders

Let's be honest. A lot of leaders in your congregation may be content just to do what they're told. (You're right, they're still not leaders!)

How do you develop leaders who are able to envision and initiate ministries in the congregation, and to manage or sustain those enterprises? These ideas may help.

If no interest or assets are available for a ministry, close it down. Tough as it sounds, this action will remove burdens and guilt from already-overworked leaders. It will also give them the time and energy to do what they really want to do.

Encourage risk-taking. Talk this way and act this way. Form your budgets this way. Don't punish people who fail. Talk about your mistakes, and learn from them. Laugh together. Have fun.

Insist on ownership in any new venture. Don't start anything only because you should or because "it's a good idea." Insist that one of the assets behind any new venture is at least one person who has a passion for its possibilities.

Limit your pastor's role. While most pastors can do just about everything, focus your pastor's energies on leadership development and Word and Sacrament ministry. That's enough.

Ask for accountability. This means telling each other what you're doing and how it's going. Blaming and shaming are not part of accountability.

ANOTHER LOOK

A PASTOR IN PUERTO RICO GETS NERVOUS ANY TIME SHE HEARS MEMBERS TALKING ABOUT "HELPING OUR PASTOR." SHE ENCOURAGES MEMBERS TO CHANGE THAT ATTITUDE BY INSISTING THAT THE WHOLE CONGREGATION OWNS ITS MINISTRIES.

Changing the culture

Pastor Bill had been serving congregations all his life. Close to retirement, he wanted to make this last call a place where "congregational culture" would reflect his commitment to asset-based approaches. He set himself these standards for the six years remaining before retirement.

Negativity and needs will be less evident.
Bill hoped for fewer people who felt negative about the congregation, and few who spoke or acted from a needs-based mentality.

Hope will be expressed in all places. A hopeful person for his entire ministry, Bill wanted members to share their sense of hope—about their lives, the world and this congregation—so that they could see and hear it in each other.

Structures and programs will be manageable.
Bill committed himself to a 50-hour work week, and encouraged congregational leaders to limit themselves to what they could handle. He would ask over-committed leaders to find replacements.

Decision-making will be simple and transparent.
Although he'd always worked in a collegial style,
Bill wanted permission-giving mechanisms to be
kept to a minimum. The council would grant more
decision-making capabilities to action groups and
committees in the congregation.

Members will know each other's capabilities.
Members of the congregation were highly qualified,
but Bill wanted things to go further. Members would
be readily able to name specifically each other's
skills, expertise and experience in church and
in their daily life.

By the time he retires, Bill expects to reach
these standards and to make this a congregation
based on assets.

ANOTHER LOOK

A CONGREGATION
IN RURAL NORTH
CAROLINA STARTED
TO BECOME MORE
HOPEFUL WHEN ITS
LEADERS SHOWED
MEMBERS HOW
THEY WERE
CONNECTED TO
DENOMINATIONAL
AND ECUMENICAL
ENDEAVORS
AROUND THE
COUNTRY AND
THE WORLD.

The "Bach church"

All congregations possess the asset of weekly worship.
Many claim excellent music as part of that worship
experience. But a historic congregation in an
ethnically and economically mixed neighborhood
in Kansas City has identified its primary asset even
more specifically: liturgical worship.

This congregation has many assets, including its
venerable history, a robust stewardship program and
active ministries in the community. But for a number
of years its reputation for excellent worship music has
been the asset that has branded the congregation.
It's known as "The Bach Church," one especially
adept at classical and baroque musical styles. This
asset has attracted visitors and members, including
professional and amateur musicians, from the entire
metropolitan area. Singers, instrumentalists, composers,
music students, teachers and lovers of classical music
all find their way to this congregation.

The congregation uses several musical styles
in worship, and all are offered with accomplished
skill and significant involvement of congregation
members. An annual music festival draws performers
and new audiences to the congregation.

This congregation's asset—excellent liturgical
worship—is so well known that it serves as
a foundation for evangelism, congregational
identity and mission.

□ **"INVOLVEMENT" IS THE ASSET HERE.**

□ **THIS IS ONE OF THE SPIN-OFFS FROM THE BASIC ASSET.**

□ **WHEN NAMED, ASSETS LEAD TO IDENTITIES OR "BRANDS."**

Funding mission 1

Stewardship leaders at House of Prayer felt that "mission funding" was the responsibility of all congregational leaders. They reserved the Memorial Park clubhouse for a Saturday morning and invited all leaders to come to this "Money Talks" conversation.

We all have to start talking about money openly, intelligently and hopefully. "Money is an asset," the stewardship leaders said, "and if we treat it as a secret, we lose the power of the asset."

We have to help each other with financial matters. The stewardship leaders knew how few families kept a budget and how many wanted desperately to reduce credit card debt. They also knew that these two factors limited families' financial contributions. They turned to financial planners in the congregation who knew how to help with this matter.

We're going to revisit what God has to say about "money" and "giving." It had been years since a sincere and sustained effort had been made to teach what God had to say about these two matters. The stewardship leaders already had some idea where to start.

We're going to increase opportunities for giving. "More opportunities" would mean "increased giving." House of Prayer members could get excited about what their offerings accomplished.

We're building for a long-term future. The stewardship leaders knew that most leaders wanted House of Prayer to be a vibrant congregation for their grandchildren. This yearning would change the way they used and saved money.

Another Look

EACH FALL THE COUNCIL IN A CONGREGATION IN FLAGSTAFF, ARIZ., TAKES ON THE TASK OF MISSION FUNDING BY BECOMING "THE STEWARDSHIP COMMITTEE." THEY DEDICATE TWO MONTHS OF THEIR TIME TO THIS FUNDAMENTAL MISSION.

Funding mission 2

Because the day ended with genuine excitement about the next steps, the stewardship leaders at House of Prayer invited the other leaders to stay for lunch after Sunday worship two weeks later. The conversation continued.

We have good reasons to ask for members' contributions. In the past there had been some reluctance about asking. But the stewardship leaders had learned about case statements from a member who worked in non-profit philanthropy, and they knew that this congregation's assets and mission were accomplishing part of God's plan.

We will increase the number of givers in this congregation, and the size and frequency of their giving. The stewardship leaders asked what would happen if children, youth, seasonal, "marginal" and "inactive" members were approached as willing donors, and given the opportunity to fund God's mission through House of Prayer. The possibilities were intriguing.

We will honor our donors. The stewardship leaders noted how few times contributors were thanked and how few of them were asked about their hopes for these contributions. THAT would change right away.

We will set up a mission endowment fund. The number of members approaching the end of their lives would increase within the next 10 years. The stewardship leaders hoped others would get excited about a mission endowment fund to help make possible special ministries in the future.

The lunchtime came to a close with all leaders genuinely interested in the possibilities that the stewardship leaders had shown them.

ANOTHER LOOK

AS YOU ASK MEMBERS FOR FINANCIAL CONTRIBUTIONS, ONE OF YOUR GREATEST ASSETS IS YOUR ENTHUSIASM FOR WHAT YOUR CONGREGATION ACCOMPLISHES IN CHRIST'S NAME. THAT ATTITUDE ALONE MAKES YOU AN EFFECTIVE STEWARDSHIP LEADER.

Money well spent

A congregation in Vancouver, Wash., distributes
social ministry funds in an asset-based way. It works
like this.

□

**UNUSUAL, BECAUSE
"SOCIAL MINISTRY"
IS SOMETIMES ONLY
ABOUT NEEDS.**

Any regular group of the congregation—including
small groups that meet in homes or elsewhere—is
considered a part of the assets of the congregation.
This includes interesting collections of people like
"the computer geeks" and the "men's breakfast group."

□

**BECAUSE OF SHARED
CONVERSATION, THESE
GROUPS KNOW EACH
OTHER'S ASSETS WELL.**

Any of these groups are eligible to receive a small
grant—limited to around $500—provided that they
match it with their own labor to affect some good
in the community. The fund that supplies the grants
is part of the congregation's total budget.
Accountability is simple: the task gets done well!

□

**NOTICE "MATCH," A
SURE-SIGN OF ASSET-
BASED APPROACHES.**

The "computer geeks" used their grant to purchase and install extra memory chips in older/slower computers. They donated them to an agency providing technology to people who are poor. The "breakfast guys" purchased the supplies for an entrance ramp to an elderly neighbor's home, and built the ramp themselves.

ASSETS: EXPERTISE, COMPUTER CHIPS, MONEY, TIME, CONNECTIONS TO OTHERS.

Each group decides its work on the basis of its assets. The congregation's gathered trust—evidenced in the well-spent money of the small grants—becomes a supporting asset as well. This program continues because it is asset-based, and because it provides a focus for small-group ministry.

TRUST IS ALWAYS AN ASSET, EVEN WHEN IT'S INVISIBLE.

Being present

The asset-based approach can reach into your community, including but not limited to your ministries of caring and justice. Here's how that might look.

St. Michael's sees its members' involvement in community organizations as an asset, and so honors them regularly and posts on its bulletin boards and e-mailings notices of their volunteer work.

Yeager Memorial has thought about commissioning members for their work in business, industry and government. In that way, these assets of the congregation would be recognized and shared with the world outside the congregation.

Beaver Creek Church targeted two community groups as partners in its work to stem the flight of residents from town. When they work together, each will be an asset for the others.

Gloria de Cristo has as members 15 educators who work in the town. They invited other members to offer the assets of their time and skills by volunteering in their classrooms and school activities.

St. Peter's by the Sea almost burned down three years ago. Every year during Fire Safety Week, community fire fighters are honored in a gala event. The congregation sees these men and women as a continuing asset.

In each of these congregations, there is an inter-relationship between the assets of the congregation and those of the community. In each case, a greater good is accomplished by their combined assets than if they worked in isolation from each other.

ANOTHER LOOK

CONGREGATIONS THAT SEE THE WORLD AS ESSENTIALLY "OTHER" WILL NEVER BE ABLE TO SHARE IN THE ASSETS THAT GOD HAS MADE AVAILABLE TO THEM OUTSIDE OF THE CHURCH.

Great Permission Glossary

ACCOUNTABILITY: The quality or state of being accountable (being subject to giving an account, answerable); sometimes a feared word, but in asset-based approaches it becomes welcome evidence of the surrounding support of like-minded account-givers.

ACID: A disposition, manner, nature or substance capable of eating away at or otherwise disintegrating a substance by its reaction with the other; sour to the taste, hard to miss. From Latin *acidus,* to be sour.

ASSAY: To examine and determine as to characteristics such as quality, weight or chemical composition; requires analysis of absence or presence of one or more components. From Old French, *assai,* a test or effort.

ASSETS: Possessions, traits, effects, property, resources, valued intangibles or wealth. From the Old French *asez,* enough (to satisfy creditors), perhaps rooted in the Vulgar Latin *ad satis,* to the point of sufficiency. In modern French *atouts,* literally "for all."

CAPACITY: Mental or physical ability, or the power or facility to produce or perform a task; also denotes the suitability (of a storage vessel) for containing a full measure.

CHAOS: Temporarily disordered reality, not necessarily a negative state of affairs; the original state of the world (Genesis 1:2). From the Greek *chainein,* to yawn. Chaos was "the yawning abyss" outside of the ordered, known universe.

ENOUGH: Occurring in quantities sufficient to satisfy needs or fulfill requirements. Sufficiency is the quality of living content with "enough." In asset-based approaches, God always supplies more than enough. From Greek *enenkein* to carry.

ENTERPRISE: An especially difficult, complex or risk-filled project or undertaking; also the qualities of character necessary to engage in this effort. From Old French *entreprendre*, to undertake.

FUTILITY: The state of being futile, having no use, purpose or effect. Because they enable achievement of realistic goals, asset-based approaches diminish futility. From the Latin *futilis*, brittle, pointless (close to *fundere*, to pour).

GIFT: A noteworthy capacity, talent or endowment; something transferred from one person to another, without reward. Known for its having been given and received. (An asset is a gift put to use.) From Old English *giefan*, to give.

GRACE: Undeserved favor from God; the starting place or most original causative notion of Christian faith and life; most descriptive of God's nature. From the Latin *gratia*, (favor, charm or thanks), based on gratus (pleasing) and akin to the Sanskrit *grnAti* ("he praises").

INACTIVES: Term used to describe congregation members who participate infrequently. Sometimes pejorative, rarely helpful and not necessarily descriptive of the daily ministries of these Christians in the world.

LEGACY: The sum of collected inheritance, both received and given across generations; may be physical (property, wealth) or intangible (attitudes, personal traits, condition). Christians receive a legacy, manage legacies, and leave legacies for following generations. Originally denoted the office of the legate, a church official. Rooted in Latin *lex/legis*, law(s).

NEED: The lack of something required, desirable or useful; denotes a deficit requiring relief or correction. From Old German *not*, distress or need.

PERMISSION: The act of permitting (authorizing or making possible); asset-based approaches are based on the authority and possibility-making of God. From Latin *permittere*, to let through.

PLANNING: To arrange the parts of a plan. In asset-based approaches, deciding what to do next together (a small-steps approach). From French *planter*, to plant or fix in place; rooted in Latin *planum*, level ground.

POTENTIAL: Existing in the realm of possibility, or capable of development into actuality; sometimes mere evidence of the capacity for possibility. From Latin *potens*, power.

PROBLEM: A question raised for inquiry (in its most benign definition), the word also names sources for complexity, vexation, distress or other difficulties. From Greek *proballein,* to throw forward (as a result of encountering an obstacle).

STEWARD: Employee or servant in large estate who manages concerns and interests of owner. Stewards are asset managers. Originally a "secular" term, appropriated by New Testament writers. From Greek *economos,* servant/slave responsible for plan *(economia)* of owner. Current usage from Old English *stywaerden,* warden of (pig) sty or hall.

STEWARDSHIP: The office, practice or obligations of a steward, who manages, supervises or otherwise conducts the business of an owner on the owner's behalf. Involves everything I do after I say "I believe!"

TIME: A measurable period during which action exists or continues; historical period or the point at which something occurs; an asset equally distributed to all living organisms. From Old English *tid* tide; akin to Old High German *zeit* time, and perhaps to Greek *daiesthai* to divide.